Looking at . . .
Tyrannosaurus rex
A Dinosaur from the CRETACEOUS Period

THE NEW
DINOSAUR
COLLECTION

For a free color catalog describing Gareth Stevens's list of high-quality books, call 1-800-341-3569 (USA) or 1-800-461-9120 (Canada).

ISBN 0-8368-1049-X

This North American edition first published in 1993 by
Gareth Stevens Publishing
1555 North RiverCenter Drive, Suite 201
Milwaukee, Wisconsin 53212 USA

This U.S. edition © 1993 by Gareth Stevens, Inc. Created with original
© 1993 by Quartz Editorial Services, Premier House, 112 Station Road,
Edgware HA8 7AQ U.K.

Consultant: Dr. David Norman, Director of the Sedgwick Museum of Geology,
University of Cambridge, England.

Printed in MEXICO
1 2 3 4 5 6 7 8 9 98 97 96 95 94 93

At this time, Gareth Stevens, Inc., does not use 100 percent recycled paper, although the paper
used in our books does contain about 30 percent recycled fiber. This decision was made after a
careful study of current recycling procedures revealed their dubious environmental benefits. We
will continue to explore recycling options.

Looking at . . . Tyrannosaurus rex
A Dinosaur from the CRETACEOUS Period

by Heather Amery
Illustrated by Tony Gibbons

THE NEW
DINOSAUR
COLLECTION

Gareth Stevens Publishing
MILWAUKEE

Contents

5   Introducing **Tyrannosaurus rex**

6   The changing planet

8   Giant discovery

10 Millions of years ago

12 Monster bones

14 Dinosaur attack!

16 Fearful predator

18 The **Tyrannosaurid** family

20 **Tyrannosaurus** data

22 End of the dinosaurs

24 Glossary and Index

Introducing
Tyrannosaurus rex

Enormous and terrifying,
Tyrannosaurus rex (TIE-RAN-OH-
SAW-RUS RECKS) was a monster –
the fiercest dinosaur of all time.

It ate other
dinosaurs,
biting them
with huge
teeth and
ripping their
flesh with
long claws. Other
dinosaurs were
terrified of it.

They would
run away if they
saw **Tyrannosaurus
rex** coming.

How long ago did
Tyrannosaurus rex
live? What
was its
favorite meal?
And where did
it live?

Read on and find
out all about this meat-
eating creature that
once ruled the Earth!

5

The changing planet

Scientists believe the planet Earth is about 4,600,000,000 years old. At first, it was just a huge ball of boiling hot rocks and metals. Slowly, the surface cooled and hardened into a crust. This crust cracked into several giant pieces that moved apart very slowly over many millions of years. Eventually, these pieces became the land and the sea floor. The rains then came to make the seas.

To begin with, the land was one big continent, with sea all around it. Later, it began to split.

This was in the **Triassic Period (1)**, 225 million years ago when the first dinosaurs lived. About 50 million years later, in the **Jurassic Period (2)**, the land began to break up further. Many new dinosaurs now appeared.

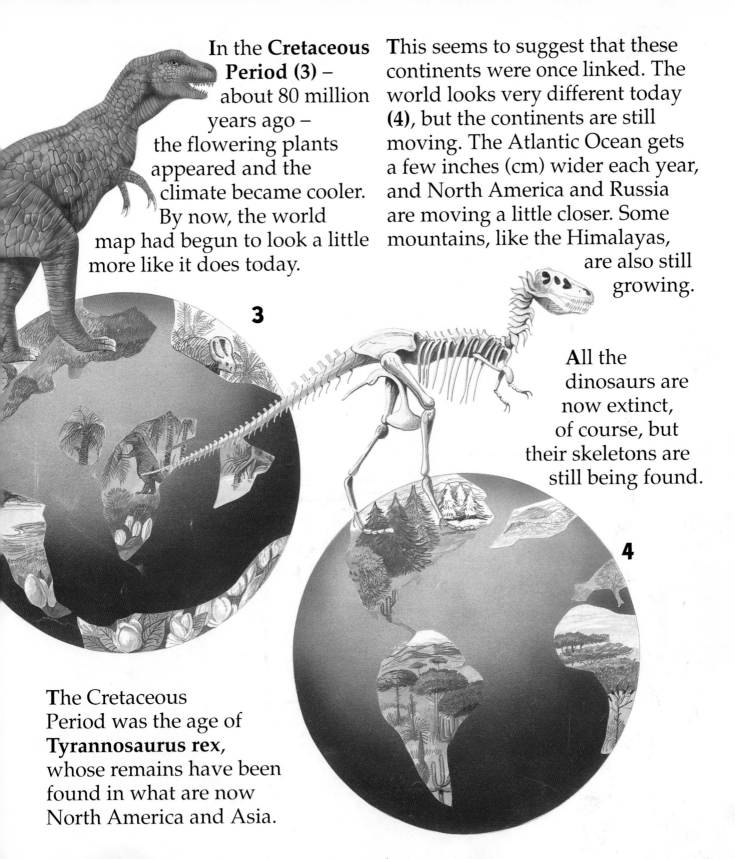

In the **Cretaceous Period (3)** – about 80 million years ago – the flowering plants appeared and the climate became cooler. By now, the world map had begun to look a little more like it does today.

This seems to suggest that these continents were once linked. The world looks very different today **(4)**, but the continents are still moving. The Atlantic Ocean gets a few inches (cm) wider each year, and North America and Russia are moving a little closer. Some mountains, like the Himalayas, are also still growing.

3

All the dinosaurs are now extinct, of course, but their skeletons are still being found.

4

The Cretaceous Period was the age of **Tyrannosaurus rex,** whose remains have been found in what are now North America and Asia.

Giant discovery

The first fairly good skeleton of a **Tyrannosaurus rex** was found in 1902, in Montana, in the United States.

It included parts of the skull and jaws as well as bits of the backbone, shoulder, hips, and legs. This skeleton was taken to the American Museum of Natural History in New York.

Before this time, many huge teeth and odd bones had been discovered. But no one knew to which dinosaur they belonged.

Tyrannosaurus rex was probably the fiercest meat-eating dinosaur ever to have lived on Earth. It was also one of the biggest – as long as two buses, as tall as a giraffe, and as heavy as an elephant. You might only have reached up to its knee!

The dinosaur had a huge head and could open its jaws so wide that it could have swallowed a person whole. Luckily, there were no humans around at the time.

In 1990, paleontologists – the scientists who study prehistoric remains – dug up the world's largest skeleton of **Tyrannosaurus rex** in South Dakota, in the United States.

The dinosaur bones were studied by a famous fossil-hunter named Henry Fairfield Osborn. He was the first to identify **Tyrannosaurus rex** and gave this dinosaur its name, which means "king of the tyrant reptiles."

But the paleontologists found this skeleton, which they nicknamed *Sue*, on land that belongs to the Sioux Indians. Today, paleontologists and American Indians still argue over who owns the skeleton.

Millions of years ago

About 67 million years ago, in the Cretaceous Period when **Tyrannosaurus rex** lived, Earth looked very different from the way it does today. The weather was much cooler than in earlier times, but there were no very cold winters – even in the far north.

Herds of dinosaurs wandered in the forests looking for food. The first flowering plants grew at this time. There was no grass as yet. But plant-eating dinosaurs, such as **Euplocephalus** (YOO-PLO-SEFF-A-LUS), with its small teeth and weak jaws, grazed on ground ferns. With other dinosaurs, it nibbled on the first oak and magnolia trees, which often grew near streams.

Crocodiles, turtles, and fish swam in the shallow rivers, while long-necked reptiles, known as plesiosaurs, swam in the seas.

In the salty river mouths, there were giant lizards, called mosasaurs. These grew up to 33 feet (10 m). That's as long as a bus.

Dragonflies and other flying insects buzzed in the air. Beetles, crickets, and cockroaches crawled among the mosses, and snakes slithered through the ferns. In the skies above flew great batlike reptiles called pterosaurs.

The very large plant-eating dinosaurs – such as **Brachiosaurus** (BRAK-EE-OH-SAW-RUS) – had mostly died out by now, but smaller ones still roamed the land. Giant meat-eaters, such as **Tyrannosaurus rex**, hunted and ate them.

Some of the smaller dinosaurs had armored bodies and tail-clubs with which to ward off attackers who thought they would make a good meal. But if **Tyrannosaurus rex** was hungry and caught them, they would have found it very difficult to defend themselves against its mighty jaws.

Monster bones

Tyrannosaurus rex was a huge, heavy dinosaur with an enormous skeleton. It walked on massive back legs, holding up its long tail to balance itself.

Its back feet were very large. One foot was more than six times as big as yours. Each back foot had four toes, three facing forward and one backward, with sharp, curved claws.

The backward-facing toe did not touch the ground. The bones in the dinosaur's feet were locked together to give it strength.

At the end of its very small front legs, there were two long claws as well. But they were too far from **Tyrannosaurus rex's** mouth to be used for feeding. Some scientists think **Tyrannosaurus rex** held on to its enemies with its claws and used its front legs to push itself up off the ground after it had been resting.

Its neck was thick with very strong muscles. This meant it could twist

and turn its head when tearing at its food.

Tyrannosaurus rex tore at its prey with teeth that were extremely sharp. It gobbled up any dead dinosaurs it found and also killed plant-eating dinosaurs that were too slow, old, or ill to run away. It probably ate its own weight in meat every few days.

Tyrannosaurus rex's skull was very large and strong. With its powerful jaw muscles, it could take giant bites using its enormous teeth and could eat great chunks of meat without even chewing. It could have swallowed you in one mouthful!

Some dinosaurs may have had eyes at the sides of their heads. But scientists think **Tyrannosaurus rex** had eyes that faced forward, helping it to focus on its prey when it was out for the kill.

Although it was big, **Tyrannosaurus rex** had

very powerful legs and may have been able to run fast over short distances. A charging **Tyrannosaurus rex** must have been one of the most terrifying sights on Earth!

Most terrifying of all must have been a battle between two adult **Tyrannosaurus rexes** over food.

13

Dinosaur attack!

Tyrannosaurus rex prowled around, scavenging for dead dinosaurs to eat and looking for tasty-looking live dinosaurs to kill.

But some of the smaller, plant-eating dinosaurs could put up a good fight against **Tyrannosaurus rex's** power.

If a **Triceratops** (TRY-SER-A-TOPS) was threatened, for example, it could defend itself with its sharp horns. Others in the herd may also have come to the rescue by charging the enemy.

So, **Tyrannosaurus rex** may soon have realized that its next meal was not going to be a **Triceratops**. And, if **Tyrannosaurus rex** did not get away quickly, it might be wounded.

15

Fearful predator

It was a warm afternoon, about 70 million years ago. A hungry **Tyrannosaurus rex** plodded through the

Which poor creature would it have for lunch?

trees and ferns, looking for a meal. Turning its great head from side to side, it snapped its enormous jaws.

Tyrannosaurus rex had not eaten for awhile and was in a bad mood.

Ahead, it caught sight of a lone **Parasaurolophus** (PAR-A-SAUR-OH-LOAF-US) quietly grazing on clumps of low bushes. **Tyrannosaurus rex** crept up to it quietly, taking care not to let the smaller dinosaur know it was there.

Suddenly, **Tyrannosaurus rex** charged at its unlucky victim. The giant meat-eater's feet thundered on the ground as it ran. **Parasaurolophus** looked quickly around, sensing danger.

Tyrannosaurus rex tore at the creature's back with sharp claws. **Parasaurolophus** screamed with fear and pain, then crashed to the ground, struggling to escape. But the battle was soon over.

After an hour or two, the victor had eaten its fill, and there was little left

It gave one strange hoot of alarm and started to dash away.

But it was too late. **Tyrannosaurus rex** pounced, sinking its huge teeth into **Parasaurolophus's** neck. As it did so, it gave out a terrifying roar.

of **Parasaurolophus** – just its bones. **Tyrannosaurus rex** now lumbered away to sleep off its heavy meal.

17

The Tyrannosaurid family

Tyrannosaurus rex was one member of a group, or family, of dinosaurs called **Tyrannosaurids**. Scientists think they were the biggest meat-eating animals that have ever lived on land.

All the members of this family had huge heads with big teeth, very large bodies, powerful back legs, and long claws. Most of them lived about 90–65 million years ago in the Cretaceous Period.

Albertosaurus (AL-BERT-OH-SAW-RUS) **(1)** looked a lot like **Tyrannosaurus rex**, but as you can see, it was somewhat smaller.

Its name means "Alberta lizard," since its bones were first found in Alberta, Canada.

Tarbosaurus (TAR-BO-SAW-RUS) **(2)** – whose name means "alarming lizard" – was another huge relative. It was nearly as big as **Tyrannosaurus rex,** but not as heavy.

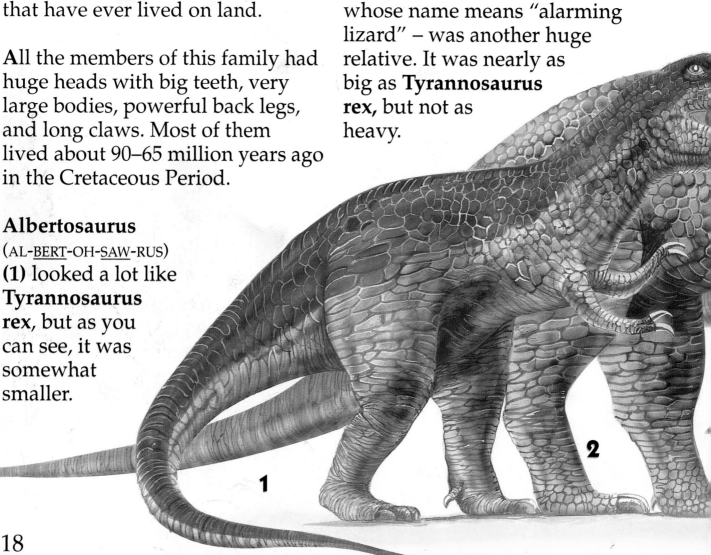

1

2

18

Its skull was longer than **Tyrannosaurus rex's** and had 27 large, knifelike teeth in the upper jaw. These would have sliced easily through any victim's flesh. **Tarbosaurus** remains have been found in Mongolia, Asia.

Tyrannosaurus rex (3) was the biggest and heaviest member of the **Tyrannosaurid** family.

Daspletosaurus (DA-SPLEET-OH-SAW-RUS) **(4)** looked like its cousins.

Its name means "frightful lizard."

3

4

Tyrannosaurus data

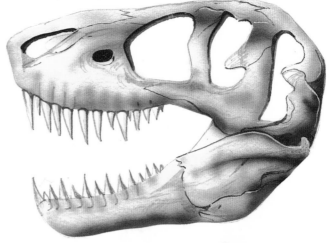

Tyrannosaurus rex was one of the fiercest, largest, and most powerful meat-eating dinosaurs that ever lived. It roamed the plains of North America and China, charging at herds of harmless plant-eating dinosaurs, killing them, and then feeding on their bodies.

Terrifying teeth

The tooth shown here is not even as big as one of **Tyrannosaurus rex's** teeth. That dinosaur had two rows of sharp teeth, shaped like this. The sides of each tooth had jagged edges, like a steak knife, that it used to tear meat. Scientists believe that if a tooth broke off in a fight, a new one soon grew in its place.

Huge skull

A Tyrannosaurus rex skull was over 3 feet (1 m) long and had powerful muscles for biting meat and crunching up bones. There were holes in the bones of the skull to make it lighter.

Sharp claws

On its back feet, there were sharp claws to attack and rip apart other dinosaurs. **Tyrannosaurus rex** had three toes that pointed forward and one smaller toe that pointed backward.

Terrible roar

Lumbering along in search of food, **Tyrannosaurus rex** must have let out roars that frightened other dinosaurs. By roaring, it could also have kept in touch with the members of its family.

Fast runner

Although **Tyrannosaurus rex** was big and heavy, it could run quite fast on its sturdy back legs when chasing other dinosaurs. Scientists can tell this from its long ankle bones.

Family packs

Families of **Tyrannosaurus rex** probably lived together in a herd until the young ones were old enough to find and kill their own food.

21

End of the dinosaurs

About 65 million years ago, all the dinosaurs suddenly died out. No one really knows why, but there are plenty of ideas.

One theory is that a meteorite, a giant chunk of rock from outer space, hit Earth. It caused such thick clouds of dust and steam that the Sun was blotted out for weeks or even months. Without sunlight, plants could not grow, and the dinosaurs may have starved to death.

Some scientists say, however, that the sea levels rose and flooded the land where many dinosaurs lived. This theory is backed up by the fact that many types of sea creatures became extinct with the dinosaurs.

According to another theory, a star exploded in the sky, showering the Earth with deadly rays. But, if this is true, how did so many other animals survive?

Whatever it was that caused the death of the dinosaurs, smaller animals, for some mysterious reason, managed to survive.

aws of 5,
20; feet of
; remains
3, 20; ta

23

GLOSSARY

continents — the major land masses of Earth. Africa, Asia, Australia, Europe, North America, South America, and Antarctica are continents.

extinction — the dying out of all members of a plant or animal species.

herd — a group of animals that travels and lives together.

predators — animals that kill other animals for food.

prey — an animal that is killed for food by another animal.

reptiles — cold-blooded animals that have hornlike or scaly skin.

scavenge — to eat the leftovers or carcasses of other animals.

skeleton — the bony framework of a body.

INDEX

Albertosaurus 18

climate 7, 10
continents 6, 7
Cretaceous Period 7, 10, 18
crust 6

Daspletosaurus 19

Earth 5, 6, 9, 10, 13
Euplocephalus 10
extinction 7, 22

families, dinosaur 18, 21
fossils 9

herds 10, 15, 21
horns 15

meteorite 22
mosasaurs 11

Osborn, Henry Fairfield 9

paleontologists 9
Parasaurolophus 16, 17
plant-eaters 10, 13, 14, 20
plesiosaurs 11
predators 16
prey 13
pterosaurs 11

reptiles 9, 11

scavenging 14

tail-clubs, 11
Tarbosaurus 18
teeth 5
Triassic Period 6
Triceratops 15
Tyrannosaurids 18-19
Tyrannosaurus rex: backbone of 9; cla
12, 13, 20; eating habits of 13, 14, 17,
12; jaws of 9, 11, 13, 16; legs of 13, 21
of 7, 9; skeleton of 9, 12; skull of 9, 1
of 12; teeth of 5, 9, 13, 17, 20